Easy Pâté Cookbook

50 Delicious Pate Recipes

By
Chef Maggie Chow
Copyright © 2015 by Saxonberg Associates
All rights reserved

Published by
BookSumo, a division of Saxonberg Associates
http://www.booksumo.com/

INTRODUCTION

Welcome to *The Effortless Chef Series*! Thank you for taking the time to download the *Easy Pâté Cookbook*. Come take a journey with me into the delights of easy cooking. The point of this cookbook and all my cookbooks is to exemplify the effortless nature of cooking simply.

In this book we focus on Pâté. You will find that even though the recipes are simple, the taste of the dishes is quite amazing.

So will you join me in an adventure of simple cooking? If the answer is yes (and I hope it is) please consult the table of contents to find the dishes you are most interested in. Once you are ready jump right in and start cooking.

— Chef Maggie Chow

TABLE OF CONTENTS

Introduction 2
Table of Contents 3
Any Issues? Contact Me 7
Legal Notes 8
Common Abbreviations 9
Chapter 1: Easy Pâté Recipes 10
    Portobello Pâté 10
    Moroccan Style Pâté 13
    Pink Pâté 16
    Potato and Celery Pâté 19
    Japanese Pâté 22
    California Pâté 24
    Smokey Pâté 27
    Cucumber and Basil Pâté 29

Green Pâté 32

Irish Pâté 34

Maggie's Favorite Fish Pâté 37

Nutty Pâté 40

Mango Pâté 42

Olive Pâté 45

Apple Cider Chestnuts Pâté 48

Granny Smith Pâté 51

Pecan and Port Wine Pâté 54

Shrimp Pâté 56

Sweet Onion and Liver Pâté 58

Nutmeg Neufchatel Pâté 61

Chives and Cream Cheese Pâté 63

Tuna Pâté 65

Blanco Pâté 67

Horsey Pâté 70

Jarlsberg and Salmon Pâté 72

- Pepper Pâté 75
- Lemony Legume Pâté 77
- Smoked Pâté 79
- Hard Boiled Pâté 81
- Pumpernickel Pâté 83
- Dijon Scallion Pâté 86
- Walnut and Cashew Pâté 88
- Sourdough Pâté 91
- Sunbelt Pâté 93
- Bacon Pâté 95
- Pâté from Denmark 98
- Lemon and Thyme Pâté 100
- European Pâté 102
- Brie Pâté 104
- Countryside Pâté 107
- No Meat Pâté (Vegetarian Approved) 110
- Seafood Pâté 112

Cream Cheese Pecan Pâté 114

Greek Style Pâté 116

Vegan Pâté 118

Nutty Pâté 120

Sweet Pâté 122

Artisan Pâté 125

Parisian Pâté 127

THANKS FOR READING! NOW LET'S TRY SOME **SUSHI** AND **DUMP DINNERS** 129

Come On 131

Let's Be Friends :) 131

Can I Ask A Favour? 132

Interested in Other Easy Cookbooks? 133

ANY ISSUES? CONTACT ME

If you find that something important to you is missing from this book please contact me at maggie@booksumo.com.

I will try my best to re-publish a revised copy taking your feedback into consideration and let you know when the book has been revised with you in mind.

:)

— Chef Maggie Chow

LEGAL NOTES

ALL RIGHTS RESERVED. NO PART OF THIS BOOK MAY BE REPRODUCED OR TRANSMITTED IN ANY FORM OR BY ANY MEANS. PHOTOCOPYING, POSTING ONLINE, AND / OR DIGITAL COPYING IS STRICTLY PROHIBITED UNLESS WRITTEN PERMISSION IS GRANTED BY THE BOOK'S PUBLISHING COMPANY. LIMITED USE OF THE BOOK'S TEXT IS PERMITTED FOR USE IN REVIEWS WRITTEN FOR THE PUBLIC AND/OR PUBLIC DOMAIN.

Common Abbreviations

cup(s)	C.
tablespoon	tbsp
teaspoon	tsp
ounce	oz.
pound	lb

*All units used are standard American measurements

Chapter 1: Easy Pâté Recipes

Portobello Pâté

Ingredients

- 4 tbsps butter
- 16 oz. Portobello mushrooms
- 2 garlic cloves
- 1/3 C. chicken stock
- 8 oz. cream cheese
- 1/4 C. scallion, chopped

Directions

- Add the following to the bowl of a food processor: scallions, garlic, and mushrooms.
- Mince the ingredients with a few pulses.
- Now begin to stir fry the minced items in 2 tbsps of butter until the veggies become tender. Once the veggies are tender add in the stock and increase the heat to high.
- Boil the mix until all the liquid cooks out.
- Now add the veggie mix, 2 tbsp of butter, and your cream cheese to the bowl of the food processor and puree the mix.

- Add some pepper and salt and pure everything again.
- Place the mix into a sealable container and put everything in the fridge until chilled.
- Enjoy.

Amount per serving: 6

Timing Information:

Preparation	10 mins
Total Time	10 mins

Nutritional Information:

Calories	221.6
Cholesterol	62.4mg
Sodium	212.8
Carbohydrates	5.1g
Protein	5.1g

* Percent Daily Values are based on a 2,000 calorie diet.

Moroccan Style Pâté

Ingredients

- 2 C. red lentils
- 5 C. water
- 2 medium onions
- 3 garlic cloves
- 2 tbsps sesame oil
- 1 tsp dried basil
- 1 tsp oregano
- 1 tsp thyme
- 1/4 C. whole wheat bread crumbs
- 1 tsp sea salt, to taste
- 1/2 C. parsley
- 1/2 tsp fresh ground black pepper, to taste
- 1 tsp seasoned rice vinegar

Directions

- Clean your lentils then add them to a saucepan.
- Pour in the stock and get everything boiling.
- Once the mix is boiling, set the heat to low, place a lid on the pan and let the lentils simmer for 22 mins.
- Now begin to mince your garlic and onions.
- Once you have minced them add the mix to a skillet along with the herbs and begin to stir fry everything for 12 mins with oil.

- Coat a bread pan with oil then layer half of your bread crumbs in the bottom.
- Now set your oven to 375 degrees before doing anything else.
- Dice the parsley then combine the parsley with the lentils, once they are finished.
- Stir the mix then add in the rest of the bread crumbs, and the garlic mix.
- Enter everything into your bread pan and top the dish with the pepper, vinegar, and sea salt.
- Now cook everything in the oven for 25 mins.
- Enjoy.

Amount per serving: 10

Timing Information:

Preparation	15 mins
Total Time	1 hr 15 mins

Nutritional Information:

Calories	182.3
Cholesterol	0.0
Sodium	268.4mg
Carbohydrates	27.7g
Protein	10.7g

* Percent Daily Values are based on a 2,000 calorie diet.

Pink Pâté

Ingredients

- 1 (6 oz.) cans tuna, drained and flaked
- 1 small onion, quartered
- 1/2 C. sliced almonds, toasted
- 2 hard-boiled eggs, shelled
- 4 gherkins
- 1 tsp salt
- 1/4 tsp pepper
- 1 tsp Worcestershire sauce
- 1 dash Tabasco sauce
- 1/3 C. mayonnaise
- 1 hard-boiled egg, sliced thin
- fresh curly-leaf parsley
- cracker
- toast

Directions

- Add everything excluding the toast, hard boiled eggs, and parsley to the bowl of a food processor.
- Puree the mix for 3 mins.
- Now get a bowl and cover it with plastic wrap.
- Pour in the puree then place a covering of more plastic on the bowl.

- Put everything in the fridge for 8 hrs then remove the pate from the plastic into a serving dish and top everything with the parsley and pieces of eggs.
- Enjoy with toast.

Amount per serving: 12

Timing Information:

Preparation	5 mins
Total Time	5 mins

Nutritional Information:

Calories	94.1
Cholesterol	60.0mg
Sodium	543.9mg
Carbohydrates	4.0g
Protein	5.9g

* Percent Daily Values are based on a 2,000 calorie diet.

Potato and Celery Pâté

Ingredients

- 1 C. sunflower seeds
- 1/2 C. whole wheat flour
- 1/2 C. nutritional yeast
- 1/2 tsp salt
- 1/2 C. canola oil
- 2 tbsps lemon juice
- 1 potato, peeled and chopped
- 1 large carrot, peeled and sliced
- 1 onion, peeled and chopped
- 1 stalk celery, chopped
- 1 clove garlic, peeled
- 1 1/2 C. water
- 1/2 tsp dried thyme
- 1/2 tsp dried basil leaves
- 1/2 tsp dried sage
- 1/2 tsp dried savory
- 1/2 tsp ground black pepper
- 1/2 tsp ground dry mustard

Directions

- Set your oven to 350 degrees before doing anything else.
- Coat a casserole dish with the nonstick spray or oil.

- Add all the ingredients to the bowl of a food processor and puree the mix for 2 mins until it becomes a smooth paste.
- Pour the mix into the casserole and cook everything in the oven for 60 mins.
- Enjoy.

Amount per serving: 1

Timing Information:

| Preparation | 20 mins |
| Total Time | 1 hr 20 mins |

Nutritional Information:

Calories	1272.3
Cholesterol	0.0
Sodium	662.5mg
Carbohydrates	84.9g
Protein	42.5g

* Percent Daily Values are based on a 2,000 calorie diet.

Japanese Pâté

Ingredients

- 2 C. broken pieces whole wheat bread
- 1/2 C. water or 1/2 C. broth
- 1/4 C. tahini sesame butter
- 1 1/2 tbsps red miso
- 1 small onion
- 1 tbsp sesame oil
- 1 clove garlic, crushed
- 1/4 C. minced parsley
- 1/4 tsp dried thyme
- 1/4 tsp rosemary
- 1/4 tsp sage

Directions

- Get a bowl and mix your water and bread.
- Use your hands to make this mix.
- Now combine in the rest of the ingredients using your hands as well.
- Let the mix sit for 8 hrs in the fridge.
- Enjoy.

Amount per serving: 8

Timing Information:

Preparation	15 mins
Total Time	8 h 15 mins

Nutritional Information:

Calories	69.8
Cholesterol	0.0
Sodium	125.3
Carbohydrates	3.9g
Protein	1.9g

* Percent Daily Values are based on a 2,000 calorie diet.

California Pâté

Ingredients

- 8 oz. zucchini
- 1 tsp white wine vinegar
- 1 tsp salt
- 1 tsp sugar
- 2 tbsps chopped parsley
- 2 tbsps chopped chives
- 3 oz. cream cheese
- paprika
- 1 cucumber, sliced thinly
- salt and pepper

Directions

- Grate your zucchini in a bowl and top the veggies with the sugar, salt, and vinegar.
- Now line a sieve with cheesecloth, if handy, then place the mix into the sieve.
- Let the mix sit in the sieve, in a bowl, for 2 hrs.
- Now begin to mince your chives and parsley with in a food processor.
- After the zucchini has sat in the sieve begin to squeeze the mix to remove as much liquid as you can.

- Add this to the bowl of the food processor as well and begin to puree it.
- Now combine in the cream cheese some pepper and salt and continue to puree.
- Place everything into a bowl and place a covering of plastic on the bowl.
- Put everything in the fridge for 8 hrs.
- Top the mix with some paprika and pieces of cucumber.
- Enjoy.

Amount per serving: 4

Timing Information:

Preparation	1 hr 30 mins
Total Time	1 hr 30 mins

Nutritional Information:

Calories	88.5
Cholesterol	23.3
Sodium	651.1mg
Carbohydrates	3.7g
Protein	2.4g

* Percent Daily Values are based on a 2,000 calorie diet.

Smokey Pâté

Ingredients

- 1 small onion, peeled and quartered
- 8 oz. softened cream cheese
- 1 can salmon, skinned and boned
- 2 tbsps lemon juice
- 1 tbsp horseradish
- 2 tsps dill
- 1/4 C. parsley
- 1/2 tsp liquid smoke
- 1 tsp Worcestershire sauce
- dash of tobasco
- salt and pepper

Directions

- Add the onions to the bowl of a food processer.
- Puree and mince the mix. Then combine in the: cream cheese, salmon, lemon juice, horseradish, dill, parsley, liquid smoke, Worcestershire, pepper, and salt.
- Puree the mix into a smooth paste.
- Now pour the mix into a bowl and place a covering of plastic on the bowl.
- Put everything in the fridge for 8 hrs. Enjoy.

Amount per serving: 1

Timing Information:

| Preparation | 10 mins |
| Total Time | 10 mins |

Nutritional Information:

Calories	1119.2
Cholesterol	372.3mg
Sodium	943.3mg
Carbohydrates	19.5g
Protein	65.6g

* Percent Daily Values are based on a 2,000 calorie diet.

Cucumber and Basil Pâté

Ingredients

- 1 can sardines, drained
- 1/2 lemon, juice and rind of
- 5 tbsps yoghurt, natural low-fat
- 1/4 C. low fat cottage cheese
- 1 C. cucumbers, finely chopped
- fresh basil leaf, finely chopped
- 1/4 tsp garlic salt
- fresh ground black pepper, to taste
- 4 thin slices cucumbers, made into twists, for garnish
- 4 sprigs parsley, for garnish

Directions

- Get a bowl, combine: lemon juice, lemon rind, and the sardines without the liquid.
- Mash everything with a fork until the mix is paste-like.
- Now combine in the cottage cheese and the yogurt but make sure to drain any excess liquids from each if you find extra moisture.

- Continue to mix to the cottage cheese and yogurt with the sardines then add in the basil and cucumber.
- Add in the black pepper and garlic salt.
- Divide the mix between 4 ramekins then top each with the parsley sprigs and the cucumber twist.
- Enjoy.

Amount per serving: 4

Timing Information:

Preparation	5 mins
Total Time	5 mins

Nutritional Information:

Calories	199.9
Cholesterol	41.2
Sodium	219.9
Carbohydrates	31.2g
Protein	14.4g

* Percent Daily Values are based on a 2,000 calorie diet.

Green Pâté

Ingredients

- 1 1/2 C. mashed avocados
- 4 oz. cream cheese
- 1 tbsp finely chopped green onion
- 1 tbsp finely chopped parsley
- lime juice
- 1 clove garlic, crushed
- 1 pinch chili powder
- salt and pepper
- chopped parsley
- 2 tbsps chopped pistachio nuts

Directions

- Add the following to the bowl of a food processor: chili powder, avocado, garlic, cream cheese, lime juice, parsley, and onions.
- Add some more pepper and salt then continue to puree the mix.
- Cover a mold with some plastic wrap then layer your nuts into the dish. Pour in the pureed mix then place a covering of plastic wrap over everything.
- Chill the contents for 5 hrs then remove the mix from the mold and garnish the dish with parsley. Enjoy.

Amount per serving: 1

Timing Information:

| Preparation | 20 mins |
| Total Time | 20 mins |

Nutritional Information:

Calories	391.5
Cholesterol	62.3mg
Sodium	209.0
Carbohydrates	13.6g
Protein	7.1g

* Percent Daily Values are based on a 2,000 calorie diet.

Irish Pâté

Ingredients

- 4 large herring fillets
- 3 tbsps butter
- 1 lemon, juice of
- 3 tbsps whiskey
- 4 tbsps double cream
- 1 dash Worcestershire sauce
- Tabasco sauce
- clarified butter
- black pepper

Directions

- Cook your kippers on the grill for 5 mins each side then let the fish lose their heat and remove the bones and skin.
- Add the fish to the bowl of a food processor and also add in the regular butter.
- Begin to puree the mix then add in the black pepper, whisky, and lemon juice.
- Continue to the puree the mix a bit then combine in the tabasco, Worcestershire and cream.
- Finally puree everything until smooth for 2 more mins.

- Divide the mix between ramekins then top each with a bit of clarified butter.
- Place a covering of plastic on the ramekins and place everything in the fridge until it is chilled.
- Enjoy.

Amount per serving: 4

Timing Information:

Preparation	30 mins
Total Time	35 mins

Nutritional Information:

Calories	447.5
Cholesterol	153.8mg
Sodium	248.1mg
Carbohydrates	1.2g
Protein	33.4g

* Percent Daily Values are based on a 2,000 calorie diet.

Maggie's Favorite Fish Pâté

Ingredients

- 4 oz. smoked fish fillet, de-boned, skin removed
- 3 oz. cream cheese, at room temperature
- 1 1/2 tbsps mayonnaise
- 1/4 C. finely chopped celery
- 1/4 C. chopped fresh parsley
- 2 tbsps finely chopped red onions
- 1 dash hot pepper sauce
- salt
- fresh ground black pepper
- capers

Directions

- Get a bowl and place your fish in it. Then mash the fish.
- Stir in 1 tbsp of mayo and the cream cheese then continue to combine the mix until it is smooth.
- Continue to add in the cream cheese and mayo until you reach a texture you enjoy.
- Now add in your onion, 1/4 C. parsley, and celery.

- Stir the mix then add in some pepper, salt, hot sauce, and lemon juice.
- Pour everything into a casserole dish then place a covering of plastic over everything and put the mix in the fridge for 8 hrs.
- Now top the mix with some capers and more parsley.
- Enjoy.

Amount per serving: 6

Timing Information:

Preparation	10 mins
Total Time	20 mins

Nutritional Information:

Calories	87.2
Cholesterol	22.8
Sodium	268.3mg
Carbohydrates	1.8g
Protein	5.6g

* Percent Daily Values are based on a 2,000 calorie diet.

Nutty Pâté

Ingredients

- 1 C. raw walnuts
- 1 tbsp minced onion
- 1 tbsp minced fresh parsley
- 1 tbsp fresh lemon juice
- 1 tsp extra virgin olive oil
- 1 tsp tamari
- 1/8 tsp minced garlic
- salt

Directions

- Let your walnuts sit submerged in water for 8 hrs in a bowl then add the walnuts without the liquid into the bowl of a food processor.
- Puree the nuts until smooth then get a spatula and remove the paste which ends up on the sides of the bowl.
- Add some salt and stir the salt in.
- Place the paste into a bowl and place a covering of plastic on the bowl.
- Put everything in fridge until it is chilled then serve.
- Enjoy.

Amount per serving: 1

Timing Information:

Preparation	6 hrs
Total Time	6 hrs 10 mins

Nutritional Information:

Calories	874.0
Cholesterol	0.0
Sodium	5591.1mg
Carbohydrates	23.9g
Protein	28.6g

* Percent Daily Values are based on a 2,000 calorie diet.

Mango Pâté

Ingredients

- 1 onion
- 2 garlic cloves
- 1 tbsp vegetable oil
- 1 tsp garam masala
- 1/2 tsp dried coriander
- 1/2 cup lentils
- 1 1/2 pints vegetable stock
- salt and pepper
- 2 tbsps mango chutney
- 2 tbsps milk
- 1 egg

Directions

- Dice your garlic and onions then begin to stir the mix in oil until the onions are see through.
- Now add in the spices and continue stir frying the mix for 1 more min.
- Add in the some pepper, some salt, veggie stock, and the lentils.
- Get the mix boiling, set the heat to low, and let the mix cook for 22 mins.
- Set your oven to 200 degrees before doing anything.

- Now remove any extra liquids and place everything into the bowl of a food processor.
- Combine in the milk, egg, and mango chutney.
- Puree the mix into a smooth paste then pour everything into a bread pan covered with foil.
- Enter everything in the oven and cook it for 45 mins.
- Let the mix sit for 20 mins then unmold everything.
- Enjoy.

Amount per serving: 4

Timing Information:

Preparation	20 mins
Total Time	1 hr 20 mins

Nutritional Information:

Calories	118.4
Cholesterol	47.5
Sodium	23.9
Carbohydrates	12.6g
Protein	6.2g

* Percent Daily Values are based on a 2,000 calorie diet.

Olive Pâté

Ingredients

- 1 tbsp olive oil
- 1 small onion, finely chopped
- 2 garlic cloves, crushed
- 1 cans chopped tomatoes
- 1 cans pitted black olives in brine, drained, rinsed and minced
- 1/2 tsp cumin seed
- celery salt
- 1 tsp clear honey
- 3/4 C. red wine

Directions

- Begin to stir fry your garlic and onions for 6 mins after toasting your cumin seeds for 1 min in hot oil.
- Once the onions are tender combine in: the honey, tomatoes, some celery salt, and the olives.
- Stir the mix and let it cook for 12 mins.
- Now combine in the wine and get everything boiling.
- Once the mix is boiling reduce the heat and let the contents gently cook for 22 mins.

- Now increase the heat and begin to stir the mix until it becomes paste like.
- Continue heating and stirring for 7 mins.
- Place the mix into a mold for serving and let it loose its heat.
- Enjoy.

Amount per serving: 4

Timing Information:

Preparation	10 mins
Total Time	50 mins

Nutritional Information:

Calories	215.1
Cholesterol	0.0
Sodium	880.0mg
Carbohydrates	15.1g
Protein	2.0g

* Percent Daily Values are based on a 2,000 calorie diet.

Apple Cider Chestnuts Pâté

Ingredients

- 1 C. chestnuts, roasted and peeled
- 2 garlic cloves, roasted and peeled
- 1 C. onion, chopped finely
- 2 tbsps olive oil, divided
- 1/4 C. water
- 2 tbsps apple cider vinegar
- 1/2 tsp nutmeg
- 1/2 tsp allspice

Directions

- Set your oven to 425 degrees before doing anything else.
- Cut a crisscross incision into your nuts and lay them onto a baking sheet with the garlic as well.
- Cook everything in the oven for 22 mins.
- Place the nuts into a towel and compress everything with your hands to remove all the skin.

- Remove the skin of the garlic and begin to stir the onions and garlic until browned and sweet.
- Top the garlic mix with allspice and nutmeg and let everything cook for 2 mins.
- Break the nuts into pieces then add in: the water, vinegar, and olive oil to the onion mix.
- Continue to stir fry everything for 5 mins.
- Let the mix loose its heat then add everything to the bowl of a food processor and puree the mix.
- Enjoy.

Amount per serving: 6

Timing Information:

Preparation	15 mins
Total Time	45 mins

Nutritional Information:

Calories	54.9
Cholesterol	0.0
Sodium	1.6
Carbohydrates	3.2g
Protein	0.3g

* Percent Daily Values are based on a 2,000 calorie diet.

Granny Smith Pâté

Ingredients

- 2 C. sugar
- 5 oranges
- 15 granny smith apples

Directions

- Heat and stir 1 C. of sugar with a low level of heat until the mix is browned then enter everything into the bottom of a bread pan.
- Get a large pot of water boiling then zest your orange into the water.
- Place a lid on the pot and let the zest boil for 5 mins then drain the water and run the zest under cold water.
- Remove the skin and cores of your apples and cut each one in half.
- Now cut the apples into slices.
- Layer your apples into the bread pan evenly.
- Top the layer with some zest and sugar and continue layering and topping with more sugar.

- Keep layering about 4 inches above the pan neatly.
- Place a covering of foil around everything then place the pan into a casserole dish.
- Leave the mix to sit for 1 day then remove any drippings and remove the foil.
- Cover the bread with 2 more layers of foil and put it in a roasting pan.
- Now set your oven to 300 degrees before doing anything else.
- Add in enough water to the pan so that half of it is filled then cook everything in the oven for five hours.
- Let the mix loose its heat which will take at least 2 hrs.
- Enjoy.

Amount per serving: 4

Timing Information:

| Preparation | 40 mins |
| Total Time | 6 hrs 40 mins |

Nutritional Information:

Calories	733.0
Cholesterol	0.0
Sodium	5.1
Carbohydrates	190.6g
Protein	2.8g

* Percent Daily Values are based on a 2,000 calorie diet.

Pecan and Port Wine Pâté

Ingredients

- 3/4 C. blue cheese, crumbled
- 1/4 C. unsalted butter
- 2 tbsps port wine
- 3 tbsps mayonnaise
- fresh ground pepper, to taste
- 4 pecan halves

Directions

- Add the following to the bowl of a food processor: port, butter, and cheese.
- Begin to process the mix then add in some black pepper and the mayo.
- Puree the mix until it is smooth then divide everything between 4 ramekins and top each one with a piece of pecan.
- Place a covering of plastic over the ramekins and put them all in the fridge for 1 hr.
- Enjoy.

Amount per serving: 4

Timing Information:

Preparation	5 mins
Total Time	5 mins

Nutritional Information:

Calories	351.2
Cholesterol	71.6mg
Sodium	859.0mg
Carbohydrates	5.1g
Protein	12.2g

* Percent Daily Values are based on a 2,000 calorie diet.

Shrimp Pâté

Ingredients

- 8 1/2 oz. cooked shrimp, shelled & deveined
- 1 1/2 oz. butter
- 2 oz. light cream cheese
- 1 tbsp light mayonnaise
- 1 clove garlic, crushed
- 2 tsps lemon juice
- 1 pinch nutmeg
- 3 drops hot sauce

Directions

- Add the following to the bowl of a food processor: prawns, mayo, butter, and cream cheese.
- Puree the mix until it is smooth then pour everything into a dish for serving or a bowl.
- Enjoy.

Amount per serving: 4

Timing Information:

Preparation	20 mins
Total Time	20 mins

Nutritional Information:

Calories	187.1
Cholesterol	152.2mg
Sodium	290.3mg
Carbohydrates	1.2g
Protein	14.1g

* Percent Daily Values are based on a 2,000 calorie diet.

Sweet Onion and Liver Pâté

Ingredients

- 4 (20 oz.) chicken livers
- 3 sweet onions
- 6 hard-boiled eggs
- salt and black pepper
- 1 C. chicken fat
- 1/2 C. vegetable oil
- 1 sweet onion

Directions

- Get your frying pan hot first.
- Then add in the chicken fat and decrease the heat.
- Let the fat get hot then begin to stir fry your onions until they become see through.
- Fry the onions with low heat.
- At the same time clean your liver then take the onions from the pan and add some more chicken fat or veggie oil.
- Once the oil is hot begin to cook the liver in batches.
- Fry the livers until they are fully done and no longer pink in the middle.

- Once all the liver is cooked add them to the bowl of a food processor in batches and begin to puree them into a pate.
- Once all the liver has been pureed add them to a bowl with the onions, some pepper, and salt.
- Stir the spices into the liver and add some more pepper and stir again.
- Slice your hard boiled eggs then top the pate with it.
- Place a covering of plastic on the bowl and put everything in the fridge until chilled.
- Enjoy.

Amount per serving: 37

Timing Information:

Preparation	10 mins
Total Time	55 mins

Nutritional Information:

Calories	166.1
Cholesterol	246.4mg
Sodium	54.0
Carbohydrates	1.6g
Protein	11.5g

* Percent Daily Values are based on a 2,000 calorie diet.

Nutmeg Neufchatel Pâté

Ingredients

- 1 1/2 C. chicken breasts, cooked, minced
- 8 oz. Neufchatel cheese, softened
- 3 tbsps onions, Chopped
- 2 tbsps dry sherry
- 2 tbsps mayonnaise
- 2 tsps lemon juice
- 1/4 tsp hot sauce
- 1/8 tsp nutmeg, Ground
- 1 dash paprika

Directions

- Add the following to the bowl of a food processor: nutmeg, chicken, hot sauce, Neufchatel, lemon juice, onions, mayo, and sherry.
- Puree the mix until it is smooth then add everything to a mold.
- Place a covering of plastic on the mold and put everything in the fridge for 8 hrs.
- Now remove the plastic and top everything with the paprika and parsley sprigs.
- Enjoy.

Amount per serving: 6

Timing Information:

Preparation	0 mins
Total Time	0 mins

Nutritional Information:

Calories	102.6
Cholesterol	28.0
Sodium	132.1
Carbohydrates	2.1g
Protein	3.5g

* Percent Daily Values are based on a 2,000 calorie diet.

Chives and Cream Cheese Pâté

Ingredients

- 16 oz. Cream Cheese
- 8 oz. grated cheddar cheese
- 2 tbsps sour cream
- 2 tbsps green peppers, chopped
- 1 tbsp red pepper, chopped
- 2 tbsps dill pickles, chopped
- 1 bunch chives, chopped
- 5 garlic cloves, chopped
- 1/2 C. walnuts, chopped
- 1/4 cup Onion Soup Mix
- 2 cups sliced ham
- 5 oz. hot sauce
- 1 dash lemon juice

Directions

- Get a bowl combine: cream cheese, cheddar, green peppers, red peppers, pickles, chives, garlic, walnuts, and soup mix.
- Stir the mix until it becomes a ball. Then place it in a mold.
- Now add your ham to the bowl of a food processor and puree it.
- Once the mix is smooth cover your cheese ball with the mix and top it with a mix of hot sauce and some lemon juice.
- Enjoy.

Amount per serving: 15

Timing Information:

Preparation	15 mins
Total Time	15 mins

Nutritional Information:

Calories	242.1
Cholesterol	60.4mg
Sodium	1126.3mg
Carbohydrates	5.0g
Protein	11.6g

* Percent Daily Values are based on a 2,000 calorie diet.

Tuna Pâté

Ingredients

- 6 oz. of drained canned tuna
- 2 tbsps Kraft mayonnaise
- 2 tbsps of drained hot pickled vegetables

Directions

- Add the following to the bowl of a food processor: veggies, mayo, and tuna.
- Once the mix is smooth pour everything into a serving dish.
- Enjoy.

Amount per serving: 4

Timing Information:

Preparation	15 mins
Total Time	15 mins

Nutritional Information:

Calories	91.5
Cholesterol	19.7
Sodium	250.9mg
Carbohydrates	3.7g
Protein	10.2g

* Percent Daily Values are based on a 2,000 calorie diet.

Blanco Pâté

Ingredients

- baguette, sliced and toasted
- 1 large tomatoes, chopped
- 1 tbsp parsley, chopped
- 1 tbsp balsamic vinegar
- 1 tbsp drained capers
- 1/2 tsp sugar
- 1 (15 oz.) cans cannellini
- 1 1/2 tsps oriental sesame oil
- 3/4 tsp thyme, chopped
- 1/4 tsp grated lemon, rind of
- 4 tsps lemon juice
- 1 clove garlic, peeled
- 1/4 tsp salt

Directions

- Get a bowl, stir: the tomatoes, parsley, balsamic, capers, and sugar.
- Place this mix to the side after adding a topping of some pepper and salt.
- Now add the following to the bowl of a food processor: salt, beans, garlic, oil, lemon juice, thyme, and lemon peel.

- Stir the mix until it is smooth then add the puree to a mold for serving.
- Top the pate with the caper mix.
- Enjoy.

Amount per serving: 8

Timing Information:

Preparation	20 mins
Total Time	35 mins

Nutritional Information:

Calories	76.5
Cholesterol	0.0
Sodium	109.1
Carbohydrates	13.1g
Protein	4.1g

* Percent Daily Values are based on a 2,000 calorie diet.

Horsey Pâté

Ingredients

- 2 (3 3/4 oz.) cans sardines, in water, drained
- 1/4 C. green onion, minced finely
- 1/4 C. plain fat-free yogurt
- 1 tbsp lemon juice, freshly squeezed
- 1 tsp dried dill
- 1 1/2 tsps prepared horseradish
- 1/3 C. carrot, finely shredded
- 30 pieces crackers

Directions

- Get a bowl for your sardines then mash them.
- Combine in: horseradish, onions, dill, yogurt, and lemon juice.
- Continue to mash the mix ingredients into the mix.
- Place a covering of plastic on the mix and put everything in the fridge for 3 hrs.
- Top your crackers evenly with the mix then garnish each piece with carrots.
- Enjoy.

Amount per serving: 30

Timing Information:

Preparation	10 mins
Total Time	10 mins

Nutritional Information:

Calories	28.6
Cholesterol	10.1
Sodium	64.0
Carbohydrates	2.7g
Protein	2.2g

* Percent Daily Values are based on a 2,000 calorie diet.

Jarlsberg and Salmon Pâté

Ingredients

- 4 oz. pate or 4 oz. liverwurst, sliced
- 4 cherry tomatoes, halved or 8 of the tiny tomatoes
- 1 large lemon
- 8 baby dill gherkins
- 1 long loaf firm bread, unsliced
- 4 tbsps unsalted butter
- 1/4 lb thinly sliced smoked salmon
- 1/4 lb thinly sliced cooked ham
- 1/4 lb jarlsberg cheese, thinly sliced
- 1/4 lb nokkelost cheese, thickly sliced
- 1/2 cucumber, scored and cut into thin slices
- 1 small bibb lettuce
- fresh dill sprig
- 1 bunch watercress
- 1/2 small red pepper, cut in strips for garnish

Directions

- Divide your lemon into 2 pieces then cut one in half and slice the other pieces into thin slices.

- Get your bread and cut it in half lengthwise then place it on a serving dish.
- Coat each half of bread with butter.
- Layer the following on each piece of bread: pate, lettuce leaves, salmon, gherkin, ham, tomato, cheese, lemon, and cucumber.
- Now top everything with the pepper strips, dill, and watercress.
- Enjoy.

Amount per serving: 4

Timing Information:

| Preparation | 20 mins |
| Total Time | 20 mins |

Nutritional Information:

Calories	454.1
Cholesterol	107.9mg
Sodium	2239.1mg
Carbohydrates	14.6g
Protein	27.9g

* Percent Daily Values are based on a 2,000 calorie diet.

PEPPER PÂTÉ

Ingredients

- 2 large red peppers
- 1 tsp freshly grated gingerroot
- 1/2 C. chopped sun-dried tomato
- 1 C. cream cheese

Directions

- Divide your peppers into 2 pieces then take out the stem and seeds. Place the veggies with the cut sides facing downwards on a baking sheet and broil them until the skins are browned.
- Cover the peppers in foil and place them to the side.
- Let the peppers lose their heat then remove the skins and add the following to the bowl of a food processor: sun dried tomatoes, ginger, and pepper.
- Begin to puree the mix then add in the cream cheese and continue to puree everything for 2 more mins until the mix is paste like.
- Pour everything into a bowl and place a covering of plastic on the bowl.
- Put the mix in the fridge until it is chilled. Enjoy.

Amount per serving: 1

Timing Information:

| Preparation | 15 mins |
| Total Time | 25 mins |

Nutritional Information:

Calories	514.5
Cholesterol	137.5mg
Sodium	656.2mg
Carbohydrates	20.9g
Protein	12.9g

* Percent Daily Values are based on a 2,000 calorie diet.

Lemony Legume Pâté

Ingredients

- 14 oz. canned mixed beans, drained, rinsed
- 2 tbsps olive oil
- 1 lemon, juice of
- 2 cloves garlic, crushed
- 12 tbsps fresh cilantro, chopped
- 2 scallions, chopped
- salt and pepper
- shredded scallion

Directions

- Get a bowl and add in your beans.
- Grab a potato masher and mash the beans until they are smooth.
- Now combine in: the scallions, olive oil, cilantro, lemon juice, and garlic.
- Continue to work the mix until it is smooth again.
- Top everything with some pepper and salt and place the mix in a bowl.
- Place a covering of plastic on the bowl and put everything in the fridge for 35 mins.
- Remove the covering and top the pate with the scallions. Enjoy.

Amount per serving: 4

Timing Information:

Preparation	20 mins
Total Time	50 mins

Nutritional Information:

Calories	67.9
Cholesterol	0.0
Sodium	3.0
Carbohydrates	2.1g
Protein	0.3g

* Percent Daily Values are based on a 2,000 calorie diet.

Smoked Pâté

Ingredients

- 1 package cream cheese
- 1 whole smoked trout, skinned and deboned
- 1/4 C. low-fat sour cream
- 2 chopped green onions
- 2 tsps prepared horseradish
- 1 tbsp lemon juice
- fresh ground black pepper
- 1 tbsp dill

Directions

- Coat one fourth of the fish and place it to the side after flaking it.
- Add the rest of the ingredients to the bowl of a food processor excluding the herbs and puree the mix.
- Now add a bit more lemon juice and process the mix again.
- Add in the spices and process them for 1 more min.
- Pour everything into a bowl and place a covering of plastic on the bowl.
- Put everything in the fridge until it is chilled.
- Enjoy.

Amount per serving: 1

Timing Information:

Preparation	15 mins
Total Time	15 mins

Nutritional Information:

Calories	637.4
Cholesterol	199.3mg
Sodium	576.9mg
Carbohydrates	11.4g
Protein	11.5g

* Percent Daily Values are based on a 2,000 calorie diet.

Hard Boiled Pâté

Ingredients

- 1 tbsp vegetable oil
- 1/2 C. onion, minced
- 1/2 tsp salt
- 1/4 C. walnuts, chopped
- 1 1/2 C. green beans, chopped
- 2 eggs, hard boiled
- 2 tsps lemon juice
- 1 tbsp mayonnaise
- black pepper, to taste
- 1/4 C. fresh parsley, chopped

Directions

- Begin to stir fry your salt and onions, in oil, for 12 mins.
- Combine in the beans and continue frying the mix for 9 more mins.
- Enter the entire mix into the bowl of a food processor and puree everything until it is smooth.
- Enjoy.

Amount per serving: 4

Timing Information:

Preparation	30 mins
Total Time	30 mins

Nutritional Information:

Calories	152.1
Cholesterol	106.7mg
Sodium	357.1mg
Carbohydrates	7.4g
Protein	5.3g

* Percent Daily Values are based on a 2,000 calorie diet.

Pumpernickel Pâté

Ingredients

- 1/2 C. diced salt pork
- 1 onion, diced
- 2 tbsps butter
- 1 chicken liver
- 2 slices pumpernickel bread
- milk
- 1/4 tsp salt
- 1/2 tsp fresh ground pepper
- 1/8 tsp nutmeg
- 1 tsp grated lemon rind
- 1/2 C. lean bacon, diced
- 2 eggs, beaten
- 8 slices lean bacon
- pumpernickel bread, slightly toasted

Directions

- Begin to stir fry your onions, and pork in butter until the onions are soft then add in half of the livers.
- Brown the livers then place a lid on the pan and cook everything for 17 mins.
- Now set your oven to 350 degrees before doing anything else.

- Place your bread in the milk and squeeze everything to get rid of excess liquids.
- Place the bread into the bowl of a food processor along with: the cooked liver and any remaining liver.
- Puree the mix until it is smooth then add in the rest of the ingredients except the bacon.
- Continue to puree everything until it is smooth and paste like.
- Pour the puree into a bread pan and top the mix with the bacon pieces.
- Cover everything with foil and cook the contents in the oven for 90 mins.
- Serve with the toasted bread.
- Enjoy.

Amount per serving: 18

Timing Information:

Preparation	0 mins
Total Time	1 hr

Nutritional Information:

Calories	77.3
Cholesterol	33.7mg
Sodium	157.1
Carbohydrates	2.4g
Protein	2.2g

* Percent Daily Values are based on a 2,000 calorie diet.

Dijon Scallion Pâté

Ingredients

- 2 (3 3/4 oz.) cans oil packed sardines, drained
- 2 hard-boiled eggs
- 1/4 C. butter, softened
- 2 tbsps mayonnaise
- 1 1/2 tbsps lemon juice
- 1 tbsp Dijon mustard
- 1/4 celery, finely chopped
- 2 tbsps scallions, finely chopped

Directions

- Add the following to the bowl of a food processor: mustard, sardines, lemon, eggs, mayo, and butter.
- Begin to puree the mix until it is smooth then combine in the scallions and celery by stirring.
- Enjoy.

Amount per serving: 8

Timing Information:

| Preparation | 20 mins |
| Total Time | 20 mins |

Nutritional Information:

Calories	126.5
Cholesterol	99.5mg
Sodium	225.1
Carbohydrates	0.5g
Protein	8.3g

* Percent Daily Values are based on a 2,000 calorie diet.

Walnut and Cashew Pâté

Ingredients

- 2 C. red beans
- 1 C. walnut pieces, raw
- 1 C. cashew pieces, raw
- 2 tbsps extra virgin olive oil
- 1 tsp chopped garlic
- 1/2 C. fresh basil leaf
- 1 tbsp Dijon mustard
- 1 tsp Worcestershire sauce
- 3 tbsps dried tomatoes
- 1/2 tsp salt
- 2 tbsps lemon juice

Directions

- Set your oven to 300 degrees before doing anything else.
- Place your nuts on a baking sheet and toast them in the oven for 9 mins.
- As the nuts roast let your tomatoes sit submerged in a bit of hot water for 10 mins.
- Also begin to stir fry your garlic on olive oil for 4 mins.
- Add the following to the bowl of a food processor: seasoning, garlic/oil, beans, and toasted nuts.

- Puree the mix then add a bit of the liquid which the tomatoes were soaking in.
- Continue to puree the mix until it is smooth then pour everything into a bowl and place a covering of plastic on it.
- Put the mix in the fridge until it is cold.
- Enjoy.

Amount per serving: 20

Timing Information:

Preparation	20 mins
Total Time	30 mins

Nutritional Information:

Calories	114.8
Cholesterol	0.0
Sodium	81.4
Carbohydrates	7.7g
Protein	3.6g

* Percent Daily Values are based on a 2,000 calorie diet.

Sourdough Pâté

Ingredients

- 2 jars marinated artichoke hearts, drained
- 1 C. fresh panko
- 2 tbsps chopped parsley
- 2 tbsps chopped basil
- 2 garlic cloves, chopped
- 2 tbsps extra virgin olive oil
- 1 sourdough baguette, thinly sliced and toasted, to serve
- 2 tbsps chile sauce (sriracha)

Directions

- Add the following to the bowl of a food processor: garlic, artichokes, parsley, basil, sriracha, and breadcrumbs.
- Begin to puree the mix then slowly add in the olive oil and continue to puree until the oil has been evenly combined in.
- Add some pepper and salt and serve with the bread.
- Enjoy.

Amount per serving: 1

Timing Information:

Preparation	0 mins
Total Time	10 mins

Nutritional Information:

Calories	677.9
Cholesterol	0.0
Sodium	961.5mg
Carbohydrates	104.1g
Protein	25.7g

* Percent Daily Values are based on a 2,000 calorie diet.

Sunbelt Pâté

Ingredients

- 1/2 C. sun-dried tomato packed in oil, coarsely chopped
- 8 oz. cream cheese
- 1/4 C. chopped green onion
- 1/4 C. butter
- 1/2 C. grated parmesan cheese
- 1 clove garlic
- 1/4 tsp oregano
- 1/2 tsp rosemary
- 1/4 tsp basil

Directions

- Add the following ingredients to the bowl of a food processor: sun dried tomatoes, cream cheese, green onions, butter, parmesan, garlic, oregano, rosemary, and basil.
- Puree the mix until it is smooth and place everything into a bowl.
- Place a covering of plastic on the bowl and put the mix in the fridge until it is chilled.
- Enjoy.

Amount per serving: 12

Timing Information:

| Preparation | 20 mins |
| Total Time | 20 mins |

Nutritional Information:

Calories	128.6
Cholesterol	34.6mg
Sodium	159.4
Carbohydrates	1.9g
Protein	3.3g

* Percent Daily Values are based on a 2,000 calorie diet.

Bacon Pâté

Ingredients

- 1/2 C. butter
- 1 C back bacon, derinded and chopped
- 4 cloves garlic, crushed
- 2 small onions, chopped
- 2 lbs chicken liver, chopped
- 4 sprigs thyme
- 4 sprigs parsley
- 1 cup button mushrooms, chopped
- 1/2 C. dry sherry
- 1/2 C. double cream
- 2 tsps lemon juice

Directions

- Stir your onion, garlic, and bacon for 5 mins in the butter.
- Now add in the liver and continue frying them for 7 more mins.
- Top everything with some pepper and salt, to taste.
- Then add in the mushrooms and the herbs.
- Stir the mix then add in the sherry and let the mix gently simmer until all the liquid has dried.
- Now shut the heat and add all the ingredients to the bowl of a food processor and puree the mix.

- Add in some lemon juice and the cream and stir the mix.
- Then place everything into a saucepan.
- Place a covering of foil on the pan and place the saucepan into a roasting pan.
- Pour in about 1 inch of water.
- Now set your oven to 300 degrees and once it is warmed cook the pate in the oven for 2 hrs.
- Enjoy.

Amount per serving: 12

Timing Information:

Preparation	30 mins
Total Time	3 hrs

Nutritional Information:

Calories	353.7
Cholesterol	337.9mg
Sodium	300.1mg
Carbohydrates	3.8g
Protein	17.4g

* Percent Daily Values are based on a 2,000 calorie diet.

Pâté from Denmark

Ingredients

- 1 lb chicken liver
- 10 oz. fat
- 1 medium onion
- 3 anchovies
- 1/4 C. flour
- 1/4 C. light cream
- 2 eggs, lightly beaten
- 2 tsps salt
- 1 tsp pepper
- 1/4 tsp allspice

Directions

- Set your oven to 350 degrees before doing anything else.
- Add the following to the bowl of food processor: onion, liver, fat, and anchovies.
- Begin to puree the mix then add in the allspice, flour, pepper, cream, salt, and eggs.
- Puree the mix then enter everything into a bread pan that has been coated with butter and place a covering of foil on the pan.
- Place the bread pan into a roasting pan and fill the roasting pan halfway with water.
- Cook the pate in the oven for 60 mins. Enjoy.

Amount per serving: 1

Timing Information:

Preparation	25 mins
Total Time	1 hr 25 mins

Nutritional Information:

Calories	3834.4
Cholesterol	2128.9mg
Sodium	5659.5mg
Carbohydrates	50.1g
Protein	119.8g

* Percent Daily Values are based on a 2,000 calorie diet.

Lemon and Thyme Pâté

Ingredients

- 1 C. butter
- 2 lbs mushrooms, cleaned and finely chopped
- 1 tsp salt
- 1/2 tsp lemon pepper
- 1/2 tsp thyme
- 1 tsp cayenne pepper
- 3 egg yolks
- 1 tbsp whipping cream

Directions

- Stir fry your mushrooms in butter for 30 mins then add in the lemon pepper and stir the spices in.
- Then stir in the salt, cayenne, and thyme.
- Shut the heat and mix your cream and yolks.
- Add about one fourth of the mushrooms to the yolk and combine everything then add the entire mix to the mushrooms in the pan.
- Let this mix cook for 4 mins with a low level of heat.
- Then add everything to a food processor and puree it.
- Enter the mix into a resealable Tupperware then place the mix in the fridge covered until it is chilled. Enjoy.

Amount per serving: 1

Timing Information:

| Preparation | 15 mins |
| Total Time | 55 mins |

Nutritional Information:

Calories	677.7
Cholesterol	358.3mg
Sodium	1235.6mg
Carbohydrates	11.0g
Protein	12.6g

* Percent Daily Values are based on a 2,000 calorie diet.

European Pâté

Ingredients

- 2 C. arugula leaves
- 4 hard-boiled eggs, shelled and chopped
- 1/4 C. plain yogurt
- 1/4 C. mayonnaise
- 1/2 C. walnut pieces
- 1 tsp Dijon mustard
- 2 garlic cloves, minced
- 1/2 tsp lemon pepper
- 2 tbsps lemon juice
- 3 scallions, chopped
- 2 Belgian endive, separated into leaves, or romaine

Directions

- Add the following to the bowl of a food processor: scallions, arugula, lemon juice, eggs, lemon pepper, yogurt, garlic, mayo, mustard, and walnuts.
- Puree the mix then lay your endive or lettuce on a plate and top everything with the pate.
- Enjoy.

Amount per serving: 1

Timing Information:

| Preparation | 20 mins |
| Total Time | 20 mins |

Nutritional Information:

Calories	588.8
Cholesterol	435.6mg
Sodium	498.0mg
Carbohydrates	35.6g
Protein	26.0g

* Percent Daily Values are based on a 2,000 calorie diet.

Brie Pâté

Ingredients

- 2 large heads of garlic
- 1 lb brie cheese, ripe, rind removed, cut into chunks
- 1/2 tsp cayenne
- 3 tbsps olive oil
- 1 tbsp hot water

Directions

- Set your oven to 300 degrees before doing anything else.
- Cover your garlic with foil and it in the oven for 60 mins.
- Then let them cool.
- Get a double broiler and heat your water in the bottom.
- Add the brie to the top of the broiler and let the cheese melt.
- Leave the cheese for 9 mins.
- At the same time remove the skin of the garlic and place the cloves into the bowl of a food processor.
- Add the water, olive oil, and cayenne.
- Puree the mix for 1 min then scrape the sides and puree for half a min more.

- Add in the cheese and begin to pulse the mix to combine the cheese in evenly.
- Place everything into a bowl and begin to stir then place a covering of plastic on the bowl and put everything in the fridge until it is chilled.
- Enjoy.

Amount per serving: 1

Timing Information:

Preparation	20 mins
Total Time	1 hr 50 mins

Nutritional Information:

Calories	1123.0
Cholesterol	259.2mg
Sodium	1636.9mg
Carbohydrates	12.7g
Protein	56.0g

* Percent Daily Values are based on a 2,000 calorie diet.

Countryside Pâté

Ingredients

- 3 tbsps olive oil
- 1 C. diced yellow onion
- 3 garlic cloves
- 1 tsp dried thyme
- 1 tsp dried tarragon
- 3/4 tsp salt
- fresh ground black pepper
- 1 lb cremini mushroom, chopped
- 1 C. lightly roasted walnut
- 3/4 C. cooked cannellini beans
- 1 tsp balsamic vinegar
- 1/8 C. vegetable broth

Directions

- Stir fry your onions for 7 mins in 2 tbsps of olive oil then combine in some pepper, salt, the garlic, tarragon, and thyme.
- Stir the spices in then combine in the mushrooms and cook them for 8 mins with a lower level of heat.
- At the same time begin to process your walnuts in a food processor.

- When the mushroom mix is done add it to the walnuts and begin to puree the mix for a bit then add the rest of the olive oil, beans, and balsamic.
- Puree the mix entirely then place the pate in a resealable Tupperware and place the mix in the fridge for 60 mins.
- Enjoy.

Amount per serving: 12

Timing Information:

Preparation	30 mins
Total Time	40 mins

Nutritional Information:

Calories	124.9
Cholesterol	0.0
Sodium	149.2
Carbohydrates	7.4g
Protein	3.7g

* Percent Daily Values are based on a 2,000 calorie diet.

No Meat Pâté (Vegetarian Approved)

Ingredients

- 1 tbsp vegetable oil
- 1/2 C. onion, minced
- 1/2 tsp salt
- 1/4 C. peanuts, chopped
- 1 1/2 C. peas beans, chopped
- 2 eggs, hard boiled
- 2 tsps lime juice
- 1 tbsp mayonnaise
- black pepper, to taste
- 1/4 C. fresh parsley, chopped
- 1/4 C. chili sauce (sriracha)

Directions

- Stir fry your onions, in oil, for 12 mins then add the peas and fry them until they are soft around 5 to 8 mins.
- Place the mix into the bowl of a food processor then add the rest of the ingredients.
- Puree the mix until it is smooth then place everything into a resealable container.
- Place the mix in the fridge until it is chilled.
- Enjoy.

Amount per serving: 4

Timing Information:

Preparation	30 mins
Total Time	30 mins

Nutritional Information:

Calories	152.1
Cholesterol	106.7mg
Sodium	357.1mg
Carbohydrates	7.4g
Protein	5.3g

* Percent Daily Values are based on a 2,000 calorie diet.

Seafood Pâté

Ingredients

- 2 plain fillets smoked mackerel, skin removed
- 1 package Cream Cheese
- 2 tbsps double cream
- 2 tbsps lemon juice
- salt
- cayenne pepper
- nutmeg
- 2 tsps horseradish sauce
- 1 tbsp finely grated onion

Directions

- Add the following to the bowl of a food processor: mackerel, cream cheese, double cream, lemon juice, some salt, some cayenne, some nutmeg, horseradish, and onions.
- Puree the mix until it is smooth then place everything into a resealable container.
- Place everything in the fridge until it is chilled.
- Enjoy.

Amount per serving: 6

Timing Information:

Preparation	10 mins
Total Time	10 mins

Nutritional Information:

Calories	162.3
Cholesterol	52.6mg
Sodium	141.0
Carbohydrates	2.5g
Protein	2.6g

* Percent Daily Values are based on a 2,000 calorie diet.

Cream Cheese Pecan Pâté

Ingredients

- 1 (4 oz.) cans smoked oysters, drained
- 1/4 C. toasted pecans, finely chopped
- 1/4 C. parsley, finely chopped
- 1 dash Tabasco sauce
- 8 oz. cream cheese
- 1 tbsp mayonnaise

Directions

- Add the following to the bowl of a food processor: tabasco, oysters, parsley, and pecans.
- Puree the mix until it is smooth.
- Now get a bowl and combine: mayo and cream cheese.
- Get a 2nd small bowl and add your oyster mix to it first then top it with the cheese mix.
- Top everything with the parsley.
- Enjoy.

Amount per serving: 1

Timing Information:

Preparation	10 mins
Total Time	10 mins

Nutritional Information:

Calories	1132.1
Cholesterol	296.4mg
Sodium	970.9mg
Carbohydrates	22.5g
Protein	28.1g

* Percent Daily Values are based on a 2,000 calorie diet.

Greek Style Pâté

Ingredients

- 4 garlic cloves, minced
- 4 anchovy fillets, minced
- 6 tbsps butter, softened
- 8 oz. cream cheese
- 6 oz. feta cheese
- 1/4 C. sour cream
- 1 tbsp green onion, finely chopped
- 3 drops Tabasco sauce
- 1/8 tsp fresh ground black pepper

Directions

- Add the following to the bowl of a food processor: garlic, anchovy, butter, cream cheese, feta, sour cream, green onion, tabasco, and black pepper.
- Puree the mix until it is smooth then place everything into a resealable container and place the mix in the fridge until it is cool.
- Enjoy.

Amount per serving: 1

Timing Information:

Preparation	10 mins
Total Time	10 mins

Nutritional Information:

Calories	1027.8
Cholesterol	316.0mg
Sodium	1901.1mg
Carbohydrates	10.2g
Protein	25.4g

* Percent Daily Values are based on a 2,000 calorie diet.

Vegan Pâté

Ingredients

- 2 tbsps olive oil
- 1/2 C. finely chopped shallot
- 5 chopped portabella mushrooms
- 1/2 lb chopped fresh spinach
- 2 garlic cloves, minced
- 1/2 tsp salt
- 1/8 tsp pepper
- 3/4 C. vegan mayonnaise

Directions

- Stir fry your mushrooms and shallots in 1 tbsp of olive oil for 10 mins then remove the mix from the pan.
- Add the rest of the olive oil then being to stir fry your pepper, salt, garlic, and spinach for 6 mins.
- Place everything into the bowl of a food processor and puree the mix until is smooth about 4 mins.
- Now add everything into a bowl and stir in your mayo.
- Enjoy.

Amount per serving: 12

Timing Information:

| Preparation | 5 mins |
| Total Time | 20 mins |

Nutritional Information:

Calories	72.3
Cholesterol	3.6
Sodium	190.4
Carbohydrates	5.7g
Protein	1.5g

* Percent Daily Values are based on a 2,000 calorie diet.

Nutty Pâté

Ingredients

- 1 egg
- 3/4 C. dried cranberries
- 1/2 C. chopped onion
- 1/2 C. shelled pistachio nut
- 1/3 C. cranberry juice
- 1/4 C. light cream
- 1/4 C. breadcrumbs
- 1 tsp dried sage
- 1 tsp salt
- 1 tsp pepper
- 2 cloves garlic, minced
- 1 lb ground beef
- 1 lb ground pork

Directions

- Set your oven to 350 degrees before doing anything else.
- Whisk your eggs then combine all the remaining ingredients into the same bowl as the eggs.
- Pour the mix into a bread pan and cook everything in the oven for 90 mins with a covering of foil.
- Place a covering of plastic over the pan instead of foil and put everything in the fridge until it is chilled.
- Enjoy.

Amount per serving: 1

Timing Information:

| Preparation | 15 mins |
| Total Time | 1 hr 45 mins |

Nutritional Information:

Calories	3171.9
Cholesterol	986.3mg
Sodium	3261.4mg
Carbohydrates	70.5g
Protein	227.0g

* Percent Daily Values are based on a 2,000 calorie diet.

Sweet Pâté

Ingredients

- 1 1/2 C. heavy cream
- 1 egg yolk
- 12 oz. semisweet chocolate
- 1/3 C. corn syrup
- 1/4 C. butter
- 1 tsp vanilla
- whipped cream, garnish
- raspberry jelly
- raspberries

Directions

- Coat a bread pan with plastic. Get a bowl, combine: egg yolk and 1/4 C. cream. Add your butter, corn syrup, and chocolate to a pan and begin to heat and stir it with a low level of heat.
- Once the chocolate has melted shut the heat and add the cream mix. Stir the mix then place it over a medium level of heat for 60 secs while stirring.
- Now shut the heat and let the mix cool.
- Get a bowl combine the rest of the cream with the vanilla until it is peaking then add the chocolate mix and stir the contents until smooth.

- Place a covering of plastic on the bowl and put everything in the fridge for 8 hrs.
- Place some raspberry jelly onto a plate then top the jelly with some of the pate.
- Add some whipped cream and some raspberries too.
- Enjoy.

Amount per serving: 10

Timing Information:

Preparation	20 mins
Total Time	22 mins

Nutritional Information:

Calories	369.4
Cholesterol	79.9mg
Sodium	55.4
Carbohydrates	19.1g
Protein	5.4g

* Percent Daily Values are based on a 2,000 calorie diet.

Artisan Pâté

Ingredients

- 2 jars marinated artichoke hearts, drained
- 1 C. fresh breadcrumb
- 2 tbsps chopped parsley
- 2 garlic cloves, chopped
- 2 tbsps extra virgin olive oil
- 1 sourdough baguette, thinly sliced and toasted, to serve

Directions

- Add the following to the bowl of a food processor: garlic, artichokes, parsley, and breadcrumbs.
- Begin to puree the mix slowly then add in the olive oil and continue to puree the mix until the oil has been evenly combined in.
- Add some pepper and salt then serve with the bread.
- Enjoy.

Amount per serving: 1

Timing Information:

Preparation	0 mins
Total Time	10 mins

Nutritional Information:

Calories	677.9
Cholesterol	0.0
Sodium	961.5mg
Carbohydrates	104.1g
Protein	25.7g

* Percent Daily Values are based on a 2,000 calorie diet.

Parisian Pâté

Ingredients

- 1 C. butter
- 2 lbs mushrooms, cleaned and finely chopped
- 1 tsp salt
- 1/2 tsp lemon pepper
- 1/2 tsp thyme
- 1 tsp cayenne pepper
- 3 egg yolks
- 1 tbsp whipping cream
- 1 tbsp herbes de provence

Directions

- Stir fry your mushrooms in butter for 30 mins then add in the lemon pepper and stir the spices in.
- Then stir in the salt, cayenne, herbes de provence and thyme.
- Shut the heat and mix your cream and yolks.
- Add about one fourth of the mushrooms to the yolk and combine everything then add the entire mix to the mushrooms in the pan.
- Let this mix cook for 4 mins with a low level of heat.
- Then add everything into a food processor and puree it.
- Enter the mix into a resealable Tupperware then place the mix in the fridge covered until it is chilled. Enjoy.

Amount per serving: 1

Timing Information:

Preparation	15 mins
Total Time	55 mins

Nutritional Information:

Calories	677.7
Cholesterol	358.3mg
Sodium	1235.6mg
Carbohydrates	11.0g
Protein	12.6g

* Percent Daily Values are based on a 2,000 calorie diet.

Thanks for Reading! Now Let's Try some Sushi and Dump Dinners....

http://bit.ly/2443TFg

To grab this **box set** simply follow the link mentioned above, or tap the book cover.

This will take you to a page where you can simply enter your email address and a PDF version of the **box set** will be emailed to you.

I hope you are ready for some serious cooking!

http://bit.ly/2443TFg

You will also receive updates about all my new books when they are free.

Also don't forget to like and subscribe on the social networks. I love meeting my readers. Links to all my profiles are below so please click and connect :)

Facebook

Twitter

Come On...
Let's Be Friends :)

I adore my readers and love connecting with them socially. Please follow the links below so we can connect on Facebook, Twitter, and Google+.

Facebook

Twitter

I also have a blog that I regularly update for my readers so check it out below.

My Blog

Can I Ask A Favour?

If you found this book interesting, or have otherwise found any benefit in it. Then may I ask that you post a review of it on Amazon? Nothing excites me more than new reviews, especially reviews which suggest new topics for writing. I do read all reviews and I always factor feedback into my newer works.

So if you are willing to take ten minutes to write what you sincerely thought about this book then please visit our Amazon page and post your opinions.

Again thank you!

Interested in Other Easy Cookbooks?

Everything is easy! Check out my Amazon Author page for more great cookbooks:

For a complete listing of all my books please see my author page.

Made in the USA
Columbia, SC
27 December 2021